Hairy, Scary, Ordinary

What Is an Adjective?

To Cal and Hannah, two indescribably cool kids
—B.P.C.

To my grandmother Anastasia, the first artist
in our family
—J.P.

adjective: A word
that describes a thing,
idea, or living being.

Hairy, Scary, Ordinary

What Is an Adjective?

by Brian P. Cleary

illustrated by Jenya Prosmitsky

SCHOLASTIC INC.

New York Toronto London Auckland Sydney
Mexico City New Delhi Hong Kong

Adjectives are words like hairy,

Scary, cool, and ordinary.

They describe, like tan and tall,

Funny, frisky, smooth, and small.

They tell us
things
are
orange
or
green,

Hot or cold
or in-between,

Leaky, Squeaky, ancient, new,

Easy, breezy,

broken, blue.

Adjectives help tell us more,

Like narrow street or favorite store,

Hilly, chilly, fast, and fun,

undercooked and overdone.

They tell us of an old black boot,

A rainy day, a wrinkled suit,

A silly teacher, giant hair,

A large cow at the local fair—

Kickballs that are red and rubber,

Spot's clean fur each time you scrub her,

Cold, dark mornings,

hot pink shades,

Young girls drinking lemonades.

They tell if root beer's *flat* or *fizzy*,

And if your street is *quiet* or *busy*,

That treats
are yummy,

shakes are
thick,

And if your
tummy's calm
or sick.

They're colorful, like mauve and puce,

They help explain, like lean and loose,

Baggy, saggy,

stretchy, strong,

Much
too short

or way too long.

Frilly, silly,

polka-dotted,

single-looped

or

double-knotted.

Words like **spunky**,

rather clunky,

Priceless, nice,

or downright **junky**,

Speedy, Spoiled,

Spiffy, Spare,

Thrifty, nifty,

bronze and bare.

·THE FOOT· MICHELANGEL·TOE·

They **modify** nouns
in ways that help tell us

If
someone's
sincere,

delighted, or jealous,

If jackets are
herringbone,
pinstriped, or plaid,

If babies
are
crabby, excited, or glad.

They
tell us
that
shows
are stupid or funny,

Of books that
are stuffy,
amazing, or punny,

Of looks that are **frightening,**

dogs that are **stray,**

of coffee that's **black**

in a cup

that is **gray.**

Adjectives help us describe when we're **tired**,

Or say when we're **grumpy,**

or when we are **wired.**

Lopsided, one-sided
ball games that bore us,

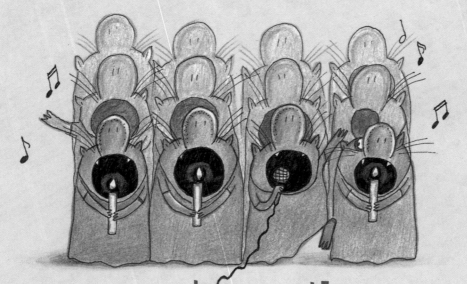

The sweet, gentle sounds
that descend from the chorus,

Mighty blue oceans and tiny red rings,

Adjectives tell us of all of these things.

So, what is an **adjective?**

Do you know?

ABOUT THE AUTHOR & ILLUSTRATOR

BRIAN P. CLEARY is the author of several other picture books, including A Mink, a Fink, a Skating Rink: What Is a Noun?, It Looks a Lot Like Reindeer, and Jamaica Sandwich? He lives in Cleveland.

JENYA PROSMITSKY grew up and studied art in Chisinau, Moldova, and lives in Minneapolis. Her two cats, Henry and Freddy, were vital to her illustrations for this book and A Mink, a Fink, a Skating Rink: What Is a Noun?

No part of this publication may be reproduced in whole or in part, or stored in a retrieval system, or transmitted in any form or by any means, electronic, mechanical, photocopying, recording, or otherwise, without written permission of the publisher. For information regarding permission, write to Carolrhoda Books, Inc., a division of Lerner Publishing Group, 241 First Avenue North, Minneapolis, MN 55401

ISBN 0-439-25384-5

Published by Scholastic Inc., 555 Broadway, New York, NY 10012, by arrangement with Carolrhoda Books, Inc., a division of Lerner Publishing Group. SCHOLASTIC and associated logos are trademarks and/or registered trademarks of Scholastic Inc.

12 11 10   4 5/0

Printed in the U.S.A.   23

First Scholastic printing, October 2000